Voices for Green Choices

Victor Wouk

The Father of the Hybrid Car

By Sean Callery

Crabtree Publishing Company

www.crabtreebooks.com

Crabtree Publishing Company

Author: Sean Callery
Publishing plan research and development:
   Sean Charlebois, Reagan Miller
   Crabtree Publishing Company
Editor: Lynn Peppas
Proofreader: Crystal Sikkens
Project coordinator: Robert Walker
Content and curriculum adviser: Suzy Gazlay, M.A.
Editorial: Mark Sachner
Photo research: Ruth Owen
Design: Westgraphix/Tammy West
Production coordinator: Margaret Amy Salter
Prepress technicians: Margaret Amy Salter, Ken Wright
Written, developed, and produced by Water Buffalo Books

Cover photo: In 2007, Volvo introduced its version of a gas/electric hybrid, the Volvo C30 ReCharge Concept. When Victor Wouk first presented his plans for hybrid technology to the Environmental Protection Agency (EPA) in 1974, the EPA refused to consider his designs. Now, more than 30 years later, the government, consumers, and most car manufacturers have hopped aboard the energy-efficient hybrid bandwagon.

The publisher and producer gratefully acknowledge the following people for their participation in the making of this book: Jordan Wouk, Jonathan Wouk, and Judith Dunkelberger Wouk for their generous donation of time and materials as well as their keen observations and insights into the life and work of Victor Wouk; and the California Institute of Technology Archive for material borrowed from the following source: Wouk, Victor. Interview by Judith R. Goodstein. New York, New York, May 24, 2004. Oral History Project, California Institute of Technology Archives. Retrieved October 22, 2008, from the World Wide Web: http://resolver.caltech.edu/CaltechOH:OH_Wouk_V.

Photo credits:
Courtesy of the Archives, California Institute of Technology:
   page 18 (bottom); page 23 (left); page 28 (left); page
   29 (top right); page 32 (top left); page 33 (top)
Corbis: Car Culture: front cover (main), page 23 (bottom right);
   JP Laffont: page 6 (bottom left); Underwood & Underwood:
   page 9 (bottom right); Bettman: pages 13 (bottom), 25 (bottom
   left), 34 (bottom right); Robert Landau: page 30 (top);
   TWPhoto: page 40 (bottom left)
Getty Images: Jason Laure/Woodfin Camp: page 7 (top left);
   Edwin Levick: page 9 (top right); Transcendental Graphics:
   page 12 (top left); William West: page 15 (bottom left); Monty
   Fresco: page 24 (top left); Carl Mydans: page 39 (top right);
   JIJI Press: page 41 (top right)
Courtesy of the Library of Congress: Image 3b21877u: page
   12 (bottom left); Image 8c20512u: page 16 (bottom left)
iStock: page 30 (bottom)
NASA: page 11 (right)
Ruby Tuesday Books: page 17 (bottom right)
Science Photo Library: Los Alamos National Laboratory:
   page 20 (bottom right); Eye of Science: page 38 (bottom left)
Shutterstock: pages 4 (left), 19 (top right), 22 (center),
   24 (bottom right), 37 (bottom), 38 (top left), 42 (bottom)
Wikimedia Commons: pages 31 (top right), 35 (bottom),
   37 (top right)
Wikipedia: museum of Toyota of Aichi Prefecture, Japan:
   page 5 (bottom right); public domain image: pages 10 (left),
   27 (top right); Richard Smith: page 14 (bottom right)
Jordan Wouk: front cover (inset), pages 1, 5 (top right),
   8 (left), 14 (left), 17 (top right), 21 (right), 26, 36 (left),
   42 (top left)

Library and Archives Canada Cataloguing in Publication

Callery, Sean
   Victor Wouk : the father of the hybrid car / Sean Callery.

(Voices for green choices)
Includes index.
ISBN 978-0-7787-4664-5 (bound).--ISBN 978-0-7787-4677-5 (pbk.)

   1. Wouk, Victor, 1919-2005--Juvenile literature. 2. Hybrid
electric cars--Juvenile literature. 3. Automobile engineers--United
States--Biography--Juvenile literature. I. Title. II. Series: Voices for
green choices

TL140.W69C34 2009   j629.222092   C2008-907925-6

Library of Congress Cataloging-in-Publication Data

Callery, Sean.
   Victor Wouk : the father of the hybrid car / by Sean Callery.
      p. cm. -- (Voices for green choices)
   Includes index.
   ISBN 978-0-7787-4677-5 (pbk. : alk. paper)
-- ISBN 978-0-7787-4664-5 (reinforced library binding : alk. paper)
   1. Wouk, Victor, 1919-2005--Juvenile literature. 2. Automobile
engineers--United States--Biography--Juvenile literature. 3.
Hybrid electric cars--United States--Juvenile literature. I. Title. II.
Series.

   TL140.W693C35 2009
   629.222092aB--dc22

2008052558

Crabtree Publishing Company

www.crabtreebooks.com   1-800-387-7650

Published in Canada
Crabtree Publishing
616 Welland Ave.
St. Catharines, Ontario
L2M 5V6

Published in the United States
Crabtree Publishing
PMB16A
350 Fifth Ave., Suite 3308
New York, NY 10118

Published in the United Kingdom
Crabtree Publishing
White Cross Mills
High Town, Lancaster
LA1 4XS

Published in Australia
Crabtree Publishing
386 Mt. Alexander Rd.
Ascot Vale (Melbourne)
VIC 3032

Contents

The Father of the Hybrid Car

When Victor Wouk first put his **hybrid** car to the test, he knew he had a winner. There he sat, behind the wheel of a vehicle that used two sources of power—electricity and gasoline. This meant that the car would use much less oil-based fuel, and that meant the car would do less damage to the planet than any other car on the road. The year was 1974.

Fast forward to Victor Wouk behind the wheel of another hybrid car—this time a Toyota Prius, a car that anyone could buy and drive. The hybrid car had found its rightful home, and the automobile industry had finally embraced his idea. The year was now 2001, and what must have left Victor shaking his head in wonder was not the success of his idea, but the sad fact that it had taken 27 years for it to be fulfilled.

Killer Gas and a Possible Cure

Gas-powered cars create pollution. The fumes coming out of the exhaust pipes include carbon dioxide and nitrous oxide, two of the greenhouse gases that warm our planet. Another of the gases is ozone. High up in the atmosphere, ozone acts like a Sun screen and filters out the Sun's most harmful rays. Down at street level, ozone pollutes the air and chokes our lungs as we breathe it in.

▲ Cars pollute: a typical mid-sized car driven 15,000 miles (24,000 km) in a year belches out 14,000–16,000 pounds (6,350–7,258 kg) of carbon dioxide.

Hybrid cars use electricity to start up and power their engines, switching to gasoline at higher speeds when that fuel is more efficient. For decades, we have lived in a world that has been choked, polluted, and poisoned by the gases that come out of the exhaust pipes of our vehicles. Hybrid cars offer a solution to the question of how we can continue to live our busy, fuel-dependent lives without doing so much damage to life on Earth.

A Frustrated Father

Today, Victor Wouk is generally considered the "father" of the hybrid car. He showed the car industry that it was possible to combine two sources of power while maintaining the kind of performance expected of a modern car. Remarkably, neither he nor his business partner, Charles Rosen, had an in-depth technical knowledge of automobile manufacturing. Sure, they had great track records in science and research, but knowing a lot about how a car works is a long way from actually taking apart and completely refitting a car with a new engine and two sources of power.

▲ Victor Wouk was an electrical engineer and businessman with a gift for spotting gaps in the market. He found a practical way to reduce car exhaust emissions using existing technology.

▶ The Prius, shown here at the Toyota Museum in Japan, became available in the United States in 2001. It represented the fulfillment of Victor Wouk's plan to develop the hybrid—a car that would run on gasoline and electricity.

In 1974, Wouk's hybrid car passed a set of tests that proved a car offering good performance and reduced pollution could be made. But the government agency with the authority to evaluate Wouk's work—the Environmental Protection Agency (EPA)—basically told him to go away.

Why reject such promising ideas? The answer is based on these three factors:

- Producing the hybrid's dual power design would be difficult for the motor industry. It would take a lot of money, labor, and time.
- Many people felt that the best route to cutting emissions was to develop an all-electric car that used no gasoline.
- The key man at the EPA in charge of testing low-emission vehicles, Eric Stork, simply did not believe that hybrids would work.

▼ A General Motors assembly line in 1973. The automobile industry's reliance on volume and speed has made it resistant to major design changes, such as switching to a different power source.

A Man of Many Stories

Victor Wouk's story is about cars, pollution, and the kind of climate change, called global warming, that is a serious consequence of our use of gasoline-powered motor vehicles. It is also a story about a man who was interested in just about everything, and loved taking things apart to see how they worked. Wouk was a businessman and a

◄ Long lines, price increases from 25 cents to a dollar a gallon, and signs such as this fueled short tempers at filling stations during the 1973 oil crisis.

The 1973 Oil Crisis

In October 1973, oil suddenly became caught up in the political turmoil of the Middle East, where most of the world's oil supplies lie. In a crisis commonly known as the Arab Oil Embargo, several oil-rich Middle East nations refused to send oil to the United States and other Western countries in retaliation for their military and political support of Israel.

The 1973 oil crisis also fueled the pressure to improve the performance of large, gas-guzzling cars, many of which barely got 15 miles per gallon (6.4 km/L). It also increased the demand for smaller, more fuel-efficient cars. At the same time came a push toward developing electric cars, which do not need gasoline at all. Wouk's hybrid car still required fuel, so it was less attractive than the idea of an electric vehicle.

When the crisis ended in March 1974, the oil pipes opened up again. While fuel economy was now a factor in car sales, the pressure to lower emissions decreased with gas prices at the pump.

teacher with a showman's flair in revealing what he had discovered.

A loving husband and father, Victor came from a poor immigrant family that valued hard work and a sense of community. In his early science work he was involved in the beginnings of television and the development of electrical equipment, and he participated in experiments that led to the creation of the atomic bomb.

Victor had a good eye for a business opportunity and liked to make money. He managed to find business pursuits that gave him a chance to pursue the many subjects of his curiosity. Over the course of his life, his business interests included electrical engineering, importing seafood, and advising on space travel. He cared about the planet and worked for years toward developing a hybrid car that would produce fewer pollutants.

From the Bronx to California

Victor Wouk was born in New York City on April 27, 1919. His parents, like many other Jewish immigrants, settled in New York upon arriving in the United States. They lived in the South Bronx, a tough, working-class part of the city. It was crammed with tightly packed tenement buildings occupied by other immigrants who, like the Wouks, had fled poverty, turmoil, and discrimination in their homeland to start a new life in the United States.

A Hard, Gritty Life

It was tough, but if you planned, schemed, and worked hard, you could make money in 1920s New York. Like generations of newcomers to follow, recent immigrants took jobs and often started businesses in fields that mainstream Americans shunned. One of those fields was laundry. Some families were happy to pay to have their sheets and clothes washed at the laundry rather than deal with the hassle of a soap-filled tub and a clothes wringer in their apartments. The city's hotels and other businesses also needed their sheets, tablecloths, and other linens cleaned.

Abraham Wouk spent years doing this backbreaking and tiring work. He washed clothes in a basement that was so warm and damp that it was like working in a tropical rain

▲ Abraham Isaac Wouk and Esther Levine Wouk immigrated 5,000 miles (8,000 km) to the United States from Minsk, the capital of present day Belarus, in about 1906. They were married in 1911.

forest. In 1925 he saw an opportunity to expand the business and set up a massive laundry in a part of the Bronx then known as Fox Square. It was to become a hugely successful, profitable business that ended the family's years of poverty. The young Victor visited it with his older brother Herman, and they played hide and seek among the piles of clothes and sheets and the hot, steaming equipment.

A Close Family

Victor was the baby of the family. Herman was four years older than Victor and would be a major influence in his life. Their sister Irene was eight years older than Victor—easily old enough to fuss over him and mother him. Their mother, Esther, was a rabbi's daughter. Like most Jews of the day, she was steeped in the traditions and values of her own Jewish upbringing. Victor's brother Herman once recalled in an interview with *Time* magazine how the spirit of hard work and love was forged in the family's traditional way of life.

"Mama was treated rather like a princess around the house," said Herman; yet she worked hard to keep their

▲ For immigrants arriving in the United States such as the Wouks, the Statue of Liberty and Ellis Island in New York Harbor were the first glimpse of their new country.

▶ The shirt room in a New York laundry. In a city of cramped apartments, laundries made life easier. A laundry would wash items and return them beautifully starched and pressed.

It Came From Outer Space

When Victor was seven, the first issue of a new magazine appeared that was perfectly suited to his interest in stories, math, and science. *Amazing Stories* was the first magazine devoted to science fiction stories. Victor handed over his 25 cents to buy tales of alien invasions, robots, and time travel in weird-looking machines.

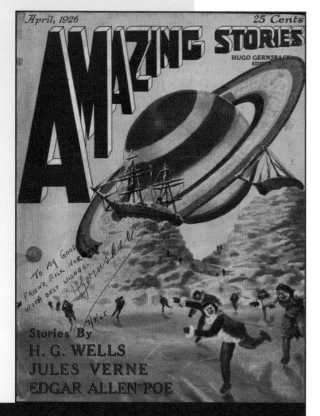

▲ The first issue of *Amazing Stories* sold 100,000 copies a month. Victor was especially interested in stories that showed practical details of how outlandish inventions might work.

home neat and tidy. And when Friday afternoon came, said Herman, "she scrubbed the kitchen . . . until the place shone. The candles were lit, and we sang the joyful Sabbath hymns and drank the sacramental wine; the children, too. My father usually talked about the Bible." The children were also taught the beliefs and practices of their Jewish faith by their grandfather.

As the family's fortunes improved, the Wouks moved three times, on each occasion to a larger home in the neighborhood where their community was based. The two boys played in the Bronx streets, although they also spent hours with their faces in a book. Reading clearly had a major impact on both boys' futures. Herman turned to a career in writing, and Victor adored science and mathematics and later said that his brother helped him learn fast: "My interest...came as a result of Herman's encouragement when I was still in elementary school. He was encouraging me to read, read, read anything."

After elementary school, Victor followed Herman in passing the entrance exam for Townsend Harris High School in Manhattan. This school offered a free education to pupils who showed good academic skills. Victor was particularly good at science and math, but all pupils had to learn two foreign languages, and he did well in French and German.

Space Man

Victor loved the high school Science Club and was particularly interested in space travel. At this time, the most famous rocket scientist in the world was Robert Goddard, who had launched the world's first liquid-fueled rocket in 1926. Victor invited the great inventor to speak to the Science Club, and to everyone's amazement, Goddard showed up, gave a talk, and stayed for dinner. Even at this relatively young age, Victor displayed an enormous interest in science. He also showed a willingness to approach anyone with an idea!

The First Sportscast

In 1935, Victor followed in his brother Herman's educational footsteps again when he enrolled at Columbia University in Manhattan. At the time, Columbia was regarded as one of the best universities in the United States for scientific research. Victor was fascinated by the new and exciting technology of television, which was then just starting up, so he chose to study electrical engineering. On May 17, 1939, he helped set up the historic first live telecast of a sports event. This was a baseball game between Columbia and Princeton University at Baker Field, Columbia's athletic field.

▲ Robert Goddard is shown in 1926 with the rocket he designed, built, and launched. The world's first liquid-fueled rocket launch lasted a few seconds and reached an altitude of about 41 feet (12.5 m). Some ridiculed his idea that a rocket-powered craft could be flown to the Moon. But the engineering behind his invention played a key role in the first landing of humans on the Moon in 1969.

The TV signal was to be sent by an antenna atop Columbia's Philosophy Hall, which housed the electrical engineering laboratories, to the main transmitting tower on the Empire State Building in midtown Manhattan. To receive the signal from Baker Field, the antenna on Philosophy Hall had to be pointed toward the field. That meant somebody had to climb up on the sloping roof and get across to the chimney where the antenna was. That somebody was Victor Wouk. Without a safety rope, he crept across the slippery tiles of the roof to reach the antenna and turned it until a friend down below with a view of the screen called up, "Hey, that's it! Leave it there!" when the television picture was clear.

The Getaway

When Victor graduated in 1939, the family recalled the arguments that had followed his brother's career choice on leaving Columbia. Herman was desperate to be a writer. His father, baffled by what seemed to him a very strange ambition, commented that if the boy wanted to write, he could pen the advertising copy for the Fox Square Laundry.

Herman took a job writing jokes and radio scripts. He turned out to be very good at this job, and earned good money and eventually went on to become a prominent novelist.

▲ (Top) May 17, 1939. A camera films the action at the first televised sporting event. The signal was sent to a transmitting tower high atop the Empire State Building (bottom). From there the signal was sent to television sets. At the time, only about 400 TV sets existed to receive that signal!

Now Mr. Wouk hoped his second son would join the flourishing family firm that he had founded, but Victor wasn't interested—and he had a get-out plan: "I could have stayed in New York City and gone into my father's business," he said. "I did not want to, so I decided I'd better get far away."

The faraway place, out of range of the family laundry business, was Pasadena, California, home of the California Institute of Technology, known as Caltech. Victor was enthusiastic about going to graduate school at Caltech because it had a reputation for great scientific research. Victor really wanted to be in a place that was pushing back the boundaries of scientific knowledge. And that place was not the laundry!

Electricity – A New Frontier

Electrical engineering was one of the most important science subjects in the 1930s—as space was in the 1960s, or climate change is today. More and more electrical appliances were being plugged in during that time, and many homes already had electric ovens, light bulbs, and the ever-popular radio sets that entire families would gather around for their evening's entertainment. It also became clear in the 1930s that a new form of electronic entertainment was about to appear on the horizon, and that it promised to be a major attraction—television. Cars and planes also used electricity, especially to start their engines. There was, however, still much to learn about how to carry, control, and measure electricity in its many uses, from car batteries to factory machinery.

▲ Inventor Philo T. Farnsworth with the world's first working all-electronic television receiver, which he demonstrated in 1928.

Chapter 3

In the fall of 1939, Victor drove across the country behind the wheel of a Model A Ford, which was developed in the late 1920s. It was a gift from his father, and he used it to travel to Caltech.

An Exciting Beginning

Cars were a rarity at Caltech, and Victor found he was one of the few people there with his own set of wheels. He said, "It was unusual for anyone, graduate or undergraduate student, to have a car." He relished its benefits: "I could park right next to the High Voltage Research Laboratory, or any place I wanted to on campus." At Caltech, Victor was a pioneer car owner of sorts—even before he pioneered the hybrid!

▶ A Model A Ford similar to the one driven by Victor Wouk (above) on his journey across the United States. Nearly five million were made by the time production stopped in 1932— evidence of the growing popularity of the automobile.

Victor was excited by the work going on with high-voltage electricity, but he also spent time in the Caltech wind tunnel researching the best shape to reduce air resistance for planes. Victor had exchanged his love of TV technology for a fascination with planes. He now intended to use his electrical engineering skills in the expanding aeronautics field. But fate took him in a different direction.

Finding Static at the Pump

One day Victor's professor came to him with an offer of work related to static electricity—a subject about which he had become knowledgeable in the course of his doctoral studies. His job was to find evidence of static electricity at gasoline stations— where even a tiny spark could ignite fumes coming up from a fuel pump or gas tank and turn the place into an inferno. The American Petroleum Institute wanted to find out if, as some people feared, static electricity was creating sparks at the pump.

Victor was offered $1,000 plus free tuition at Caltech to investigate the problem. He developed

Static Electricity

An important part of Victor's work as a graduate student at Caltech was with static electricity, also known as electrostatics. Static electricity is created when electric charges build up on the surface of a material. It makes objects attract one another and can cause a spark to jump between them. One well-known example of static electricity is the spark that makes your hand tingle when you touch a door knob or some other metal surface. Other examples include "flyaway hair" and static cling, which occurs when the surface of plastic wrap sticks together or clothing sticks to itself.

◄ When static electricity builds up, it tries to get away, in this case making the girl's hair stand up on end. It's the sort of performance that Victor loved when demonstrating the behavior of electricity.

Spreading His Wings

Victor seized the chance to learn to fly planes while he was at Caltech through the Civilian Pilot Training Program (CPTP). In this program, college students were given basic pilot training. It was begun by President Franklin D. Roosevelt in 1938 in response to growing world tensions and the prospect of the United States being drawn into World War II in Europe and Asia. The students could use these skills in a war if called upon. In addition to being fun, Victor felt this training would help him in his future aeronautics career. It was a good value, too. As he later said, "All I paid was $25 for some work books . . . and I got good pilot training." Later, when he had children, they also took flying lessons.

special equipment for measuring small amounts of electricity and put together some experiments to see whether filling the car with gas, or driving the car, actually created static electricity.

After many days of crawling around gasoline stations, and months of checking and analyzing his results, Victor decided that fires were far more likely to be started by a carelessly thrown match than by tiny amounts of static electricity from a car.

The combination of an understanding of electricity, clear thinking that challenged what people believed, and the ability to devise a test to find new information impressed Victor's colleagues. Victor would use these skills throughout his life's work, including his later work on the hybrid car. While at Caltech, his research into static electricity would later earn him his doctorate, or Ph.D., and along with it the title of Dr. Victor Wouk.

The Spark of True Love

On June 15, 1941, Victor married Joy Lattman, who had been a student one year behind him at Barnard College, which is affiliated with Columbia. For their honeymoon, they cruised cross-country in a wedding gift from Victor's father—a 1937 Chevrolet, one of the most stylish cars of the time.

◀ The Civilian Pilot Training Program aimed to train 20,000 student pilots every year. This group was pictured at Rockville, Maryland, in 1941.

What a Drag!

Victor was good at spotting opportunities for doing scientific research. Even on his honeymoon, he could not resist a chance to carry out an experiment into static electricity—especially as he had a willing assistant in the form of his wife. In the 1930s and 1940s, gasoline trucks would trail behind them a chain that was supposed to carry any static electric charge from the truck and release it onto the road surface. The chains frequently broke, and it was calculated that they cost $1.3 million a year to supply, fix, or replace—an enormous amount of money at the time.

Victor wanted to know if that fortune was being wasted. "I had the idea that if Joy drove the car and I had a drag chain," he said, "I could measure the current." Victor's experiments, begun on his honeymoon with his new bride at the wheel and him hanging out of the rear seat, showed that the drag chains had no effect at all on releasing the static charge and were a waste of time and money.

By proving that drag chains didn't work, he saved the gasoline industry millions of dollars in buying pointless equipment—and probably saved countless more dollars spent on road and automotive repairs.

▲ "We got a 1937 Chevrolet coupe [like the one shown below] that we drove across the country in and had a great wild time on the honeymoon," recalled Victor, shown here with his wife, Joy.

> "We would have a long wire, and we would put on the wire a bunch of little pieces of paper. The lightning stroke would go to that wire and blow it up, disintegrate it by the heat, and then all the little sheets of paper would come floating down and we'd get a lot of applause."
>
> -Victor Wouk, on his "performances" at Caltech demonstrating the power of electricity

For My Next Trick …

Every year the general public was invited to Caltech to see demonstrations of the work going on there. Some of these demonstrations were pretty dull and Victor, the showman, relished the chance to get a crowd excited. During one performance, Victor generated fake lightning using three million volts of electricity—a huge amount of power especially for the time. He even put on a smaller-scale demonstration to show groups of students the power of electricity.

The Spark of an Idea

Victor taught undergraduate students in subjects other than electrical engineering. He was a popular teacher because his lessons were fun and showed how the ideas he and his students were using worked in the real world. "It was a lot of fun," he said. "I never had anyone complain that the course was dull or say, 'Gee, why do I have to take this?'"

▶ Victor Wouk used powerful high-voltage equipment like that shown here at the Caltech High Voltage Research Laboratory to create dramatic giant sparks above the heads of the crowd.

Victor's methods were similar to those of Professor Fred Lindvall, one of his own teachers at Caltech. Professor Lindvall told stories and jokes during his lectures to keep his students interested. One of the stories that Professor Lindvall told in class would have a profound influence on Victor and his future work on electric and hybrid cars.

Trolley Tale

Besides being an interesting tale, Professor Lindvall's story provided an explanation of how energy can be reused, and it was later to prove vital to the success of the hybrid. Victor later explained: "His family lived at the end of a trolley line, up a rather steep and long hill. It was so far away from the generating station and so much current was being drawn going up a hill that the voltage would drop . . . and the trolley car would stop."

"But if there was a trolley coming down," Victor went on, "instead of using mechanical brakes to slow your trolley down, the motor would be turned into a generator by switching some leads, and the generator voltage would go into the overhead wires and that current would go into a trolley down at the bottom and help get it up. This impressed me enormously."

The process described here was called regenerative braking, and it is used in the hybrid cars on the roads today. The story of the trolleys on the steep hill could be said to be the spark that ignited the idea of the modern hybrid car.

▲ When these San Francisco cable cars go downhill, energy from their braking system is transferred to cars coming up. Victor Wouk used the idea in his hybrid car.

> *"Victor Wouk is on a project which may result in the shortening of the war, and I would appreciate it if you defer him."*
>
> - President Franklin D. Roosevelt, in a letter requesting that Victor Wouk be kept out of the military in order to work on the Manhattan Project

▶ One result of the Manhattan Project was this bomb, code-named "Little Boy," that was dropped on the Japanese city of Hiroshima on August 6, 1945. The bomb used a nuclear chain reaction to produce a huge amount of energy in an explosion that destroyed the city and killed about 140,000 people. The devastating impact of this and a second bomb on Nagasaki is credited with finally ending World War II.

A Top-Secret Project

On leaving Caltech in 1941, Victor was offered jobs by three scientific research firms. He took the one that paid best—$55 a week—for Westinghouse in Pittsburgh. This major research organization had invented a machine that used a vacuum (a container with no air) to change electrical current. Victor had used the device for years, and his job would now be to try to improve it.

After he got to Westinghouse, however, Victor was soon given a completely different, and totally secret, task. The war that had been threatened was now underway as World War II, and with it a race to develop the most powerful weapon in history—the atomic bomb. The U.S. research program to develop the bomb was known as the Manhattan Project and involved many scientists. Westinghouse was doing research on uranium by putting it in a vacuum and running electricity through it.

Victor's work was so vital that he was twice called up for military service to fight in the war and then told it was more important that he stay on at the laboratory. Eventually, the Manhattan Project

resulted in the dropping of the atomic bombs that devastated the Japanese cities of Hiroshima and Nagasaki—and ended World War II.

Wouk Sets Off to Work

With the war over in 1945, Victor was free to follow a business career. Over the next two decades, Victor developed and ran various businesses, but he never stayed in the same place for long. He would have an idea, develop it, show that it worked, and sell it and move on to other projects.

Victor was always looking for ways to do things better, and he had a good eye for a business opportunity, just as his father had with his laundry in the Bronx. In 1946, for example, he formed his first company, the Beta Electric Corporation, which became a leading manufacturer of high-voltage power supplies and test equipment. He sold this highly successful business ten years later to a firm called Sorensen and became chief engineer for its power supply division.

In 1959, he spotted another opportunity and formed the Electronic Energy Conversion Corporation, making lightweight but highly efficient equipment for controlling power supply. His equipment was used in many fields, such as military planes and the newly developing computer industry. The equipment was popular because it was reliable and lightweight (a particularly useful feature for its use in planes).

▲ Victor's work at his Beta Electric Corporation involved making testing equipment for high-voltage power supplies. Few other electrical engineers could match Victor's experience and skills.

Victor the Lobsterman

Victor even applied his business skills to importing seafood. Another branch of the Wouk family, based in South Africa, supplied lobster tails. In the late 1940s, Victor became president of Wouka Industries and helped run the company.

Victor and Joy had started a family and now had two sons—Jonathan, born in May 1944, and Jordan, born in October 1948. Victor worked very hard, often bringing work home and sometimes traveling on business. He tried to make it home for dinner and would listen proudly to his sons' conversations. During these conversations, he would draw upon the Eastern European Jewish method called teaching and dispute, challenging the boys on possible factual errors, sending them into the next room to check on information in reference books, and sharing their pride when they reported that they were correct.

By this time in his life, many people would come to Victor when they faced problems having to do with electrical power equipment. Some of these people came from the automobile industry. And so it happened that in 1962 he was approached by an engineer named Russell Feldman. Feldman was concerned about air pollution, and he had a question to ask that would change Victor's life.

▶ Vacuum tube circuit boards like this were a part of popular radio kit projects in the 1950s.

Batteries Not Included

▲ When Victor Wouk helped figure out why an electric car produced in 1959 (right) had failed, he came up with a plan that led to the modern hybrid. The electric car, which was called the Henney Kilowatt and had a battery-powered engine, used the body of the Renault Dauphine, a new and popular car from France.

Russell Feldman was a founder of Motorola, the firm that had produced one of the best car radios in the 1930s. Now his pet project, an electric car launched in 1959, was in trouble. The car was performing badly and Feldman needed to know whether it was worth putting in the work to improve it.

Smog—A Killer in the Air

Different versions of an electric automobile had come and gone since the late 1800s. Feldman's interest in reviving the electric car was spurred by a condition that can be described in one word: *smog*. A blend of "smoke" and "fog," smog is a thick, heavy haze of air pollution that hangs over many areas.

Smog can be deadly, particularly to people with breathing problems. In 1953, smog killed between 170 and 260 people in New York, and in 1954 the schools and factories of Los Angeles were shut down for almost a month because the city was shrouded in it.

Caused by pollution coming out of the chimneys of factories and the exhaust pipes of the cars that jammed city roads, smog was a bad problem that was getting worse. California would introduce laws to limit the amount of pollution that was allowed in the air (although it was very hard to control), and on the national level Congress would pass the Clean Air Act. Still, it was a long time before environmental issues like this were understood or taken seriously.

No Gas, No Pollution

Victor Wouk recalled of his 1962 meeting with Feldman: "He came to see me and said, 'Electric cars are going to be necessary. The air pollution is terrible.'" The beauty of the electric car was that it had no internal combustion engine, so it didn't burn gasoline or produce poisonous exhaust gas.

But Feldman had problems. The car he had developed was clearly not suitable for ordinary, everyday use. It took ages to reach its top speed of 40 miles (64 km) per hour and could only travel about 40 miles (64 km) before the batteries needed recharging. He had managed to increase both figures by about 50 percent when he came to Victor.

▲ A conductor guides a bus through smog-enshrouded London in 1952. The Great Smog of London killed four thousand people in a few days and twice that many from side effects in the following months.

▶ In the car culture of the 1950s and 1960s, big was beautiful, and most Americans were barely aware of the damage that exhaust spewed by their cars was doing to their lungs and the planet.

Victor summed up its problems simply: "It couldn't go very far and it couldn't go very fast."

A car that lacks acceleration isn't just slow when the light turns green. It also takes time to accelerate in order to pass other vehicles or avoid obstructions. Slowness can actually be dangerous.

Only some of the cars developed were used by electric companies for their staff to drive between houses to read the meter. Even for this limited usage, they weren't doing well. The project was in trouble.

Energy Gap

Victor agreed to test the car to see how he could help. After putting it through its paces, he figured that the problem was not with the car's equipment. It was "just that the batteries didn't have enough energy to take the car far or fast," and the batteries available at the time would not be able to power a car properly. When he heard this news, a disappointed Feldman abandoned the Henney car, and it became a museum exhibit.

Early Electric Cars

Electric vehicles had been around since the 1830s—50 years before the invention of the car. Scottish inventor Robert Anderson made a simple electric carriage sometime between 1832 and 1839. In 1835 an American inventor, Thomas Davenport, built a small electric locomotive. The first successful electric automobile in the United States appeared in 1891, and eight years later electric taxis were rolling along the streets of New York. By this time, nearly one-third of the cars in the United States were powered by electricity. The cars young Victor Wouk saw on the streets of New York in the 1920s, however, were all powered by gasoline.

◀ The driver of this electric-powered racing vehicle is welcomed at the finish line by a group of fans in 1889. This vehicle was reported to attain a speed of over 60 miles (100 km) per hour.

By 1962 Victor was working for Gulton Industries, who had bought his Electronic Energy Conversion Corporation. "One day Dr. Gulton called everybody in...and said, 'I want more applications for nickel-cadmium batteries that we are now building for the air force.'" These were a new type of high-power battery able to provide enough instant power to start up a jet engine. Was this the answer for the electric car?

At Victor's suggestion, a large American Motors station wagon was converted to run from batteries. The speed-control equipment he designed gave it good acceleration, but there was still a problem with the car's range. It couldn't go far without recharging the batteries.

What If . . .

Victor knew all about pollution and the toxins that came out of car exhaust. In 1964 he helped found a

▲ Around the time that Victor Wouk was figuring out a plan that would lead to the modern-day hybrid, many automobile manufacturers were trying to develop their own electric cars. There was even a coast-to-coast "Great Electric Car Race" in 1968, which Victor helped plan. The race pitted Caltech's student-built 1958 VW bus against a 1968 Chevy Corvair from the Massachusetts Institute of Technology (MIT). The VW won with a time of 210 hours—30 minutes faster than the Corvair.

▶ Victor (with arm extended) poses with the electric station wagon he worked on. The idea of the car was appealing, but it needed recharging too often.

group called Citizens for Clean Air, which campaigned against air pollution. He was delighted when new legislation was passed to make cars that emitted fewer poisonous gases. The government also set up a new body, the Environmental Protection Agency (EPA), to try to clean up America. Part of its role was to enforce the 1970 Clean Air Act, which set a deadline of 1976 to reduce damaging car emissions by 90 percent. It was a very ambitious target.

Many people thought this would spur development of electric cars, but Victor Wouk, who probably knew more about the technology than anyone else, was certain they would not work. He said: "It isn't the smart controls, it isn't this, that and the other thing, . . . it's the battery."

He knew that the batteries had to be about eight times more powerful to compete with a conventional car, and he knew how difficult that would be to develop. It caused a lot of argument. "I was actually being accused of being anti-electric car!" he recalled. "I'd say 'It's not that I don't want electric cars, I want cars that will work.'"

Victor was starting to think the unthinkable: electric cars were not the way forward. They were sluggish, and their batteries needed frequent charging. But what about a car that had two sources of power: electricity and gasoline? This would produce a low-emitting vehicle with good performance that could be driven long distances without the problem of finding somewhere to charge the battery.

Was this the way to save fuel and cut emissions without losing performance? He had to find out.

Hybrids in History
Strange as it may seem, the hybrid was not a new idea. There had been "dual power," or hybrid, cars before. Ferdinand Porsche designed the Mixte (shown above) in 1898 using the revolutionary idea of electric motors in the wheel hubs. In 1915 the Woods Motor Vehicle, built in Chicago, used an electric motor at low speeds and switched to a gasoline engine above 15 miles (24 km) per hour. The company made about 600 of these dual power cars. But improvements to the gasoline engine gave it a superior performance, and the dual power was pretty much forgotten.

Chapter 5

The Invention of the Hybrid

Victor was convinced that a hybrid car could meet the low-emissions target. "I always said the hybrid is the way to go if we must reduce automobile pollution and reduce automobile fuel consumption a large amount in a short period of time," he said. He was also taking into account the need for the car to carry as many passengers and as much luggage as a conventional car, and the rows of big, heavy electric batteries took up too much space.

Victor was thrilled when he heard that there was a chance he could develop such a car. The Environmental Protection Agency had a program called the Federal Clean Car Incentive Program (FCCIP). This program offered money for developing a car that met the very low emissions standards set by the Clean Air Act. He teamed up with a colleague, Charlie Rosen, to develop a hybrid.

The Birth of a Company

The FCCIP did not offer money up front. Applicants had to convince the EPA that they had a workable plan. This put off some people because creating new vehicles is not a cheap business. "What we were asking for was the privilege of building this vehicle at our own expense and having it tested at our own expense to prove that it would beat the 1976

▲ Victor in 1974 sitting in a tiny electric car made by Citicar. About 2,500 of these were produced, but they were a flop. They were small, poorly made, and unsafe in collisions.

requirements on emissions," said Victor. Using their own funds and money from investors (who included Victor's brother Herman), they raised about $300,000 and put together a new company to make a hybrid car.

"I didn't know what to call it," recalled Victor. "Herman came up with the idea. He said 'You use petroleum; you use electric—so, Petro-Electric Motors. And 'Ltd'— Limited—which makes it sound very fancy.'" And so PEM was born.

The two partners spent a year putting together their proposal, working from Charles' garage in Teaneck, New Jersey. They set a date for meeting with the EPA and presented their proposal.

The Go-Ahead

It took an agonizing wait of three months to get an answer, but when it came, it was yes. The EPA was prepared to consider PEM's hybrid car for its FCCIP scheme. Also accepted were an electric car, a diesel car, and a proposal for an exhaust filter, none from major players in the automotive industry.

The deal was that if the proposals beat the emissions targets, the EPA would buy ten prototype cars at a good price ($30,000) and test them for a year. If they were still performing well, the government would buy another 350 for more testing, paying double the going rate for cars. This would pay for the time and expense of developing the vehicle—if it was successful.

▲ The contract between PEM and the EPA for Victor and his business partner, Charles Rosen, to work on plans for a variety of fuel-efficient cars, including the hybrid.

'68 Buick Skylark. It talks your language.

▲ A billboard advertising a car from the same generation as the one used to make the hybrid.

Muscle Cars

It seems pretty ironic that the vehicle Wouk chose to make a car with low emissions was one of the biggest gas-guzzlers of its time. Through the 1960s, some of the most popular cars were "supercars," or "muscle cars." These two-door cars were aimed at younger drivers and were all about high performance, especially acceleration, and the roar of the engine. The model Wouk used came toward the end of the trend and was not as powerful as earlier muscle cars. But it still packed a mean punch—and guzzled a lot of gas.

Checking Under the Hood

Now they needed a car to take apart and put together as a hybrid. Victor and Charles went around to New York car showrooms to make their choice. Most car shoppers consider the style and color of the car as well as its performance. Not these two. Victor wanted as much space as possible to store the electronics: "I looked under the hoods. Not knowing exactly how much (space) we were going to need, I wanted a car with the largest volume under the hood, and it was a Buick Skylark."

But the salesman couldn't sell him the car. The model had just been discontinued and nothing was available. Victor contacted the manufacturer, General Motors. They arranged for him to receive one of the last models made, and $2,700 came out of his budget for a car that he was going to take apart and put together again.

Small Is Beautiful

Now they had to replace the engine, taking out the high performance V8, to save space.

"I didn't know how much electronics I would have to put under the hood or how big an electric motor, so I wanted something that was squat," said Victor. He chose a Wankel engine from Japanese car maker Mazda, because it took up half the space of the V8 and still offered a powerful performance.

Using Charles' garage in Teaneck as a workshop, the two partners got to work. Victor described building the car as "a long, uphill struggle because I'm not an automotive engineer, nor is Dr. Rosen." But they managed to squeeze eight lead-acid batteries under the hood and installed a system to blend the drive power from these and the gasoline engine. This required much new welding of the bodywork, and the car clattered so much that on test drives, Victor didn't push beyond 85 miles per hour (137 km/h) because the rattling was so loud.

Energy Transfer

That lecture about trolleys from years ago must have echoed in Victor's head as he set up the batteries to recharge with energy taken from the car's braking action. This regenerative braking process was crucial to ensuring that the battery had a longer life and the car did not have to stop frequently to be plugged into an electrical supply.

Finally, they were able to put on the road a working car that seemed to meet the requirements of the FCCIP scheme. They did some tests and spent an extra month dealing with technical problems that were causing variations in the gas emissions.

▲ An early Mazda rotary engine like the one used by Victor Wouk. Developed in the 1960s, this engine was small and light but delivered plenty of power. It was exactly what he needed because the batteries in his car added so much weight and took up lots of space.

"I got a phone call saying Mazda liked the idea and they were going to send me two engines, [in case] something didn't work well on the first engine... Well, I was absolutely flabbergasted!"

- Victor Wouk's reaction when he found out that the engine for his hybrid would not cost him anything

31

They contacted the EPA to say that the car was ready for testing, but the response was like a bombshell. All the other candidates had dropped out, and the EPA now wanted to end the program without even testing Victor's car. Indeed, Victor joked that the scheme was such a closely guarded secret that more people were aware of the highly confidential atomic bomb Manhattan Project during World War II than knew of the FCCIP.

Dead Set Against It

Not one to give up easily, Wouk enlisted the help of his brother Herman and contacted the National Science Foundation (NSF), a government agency that supports scientific research. The NSF was appalled that the car might not even be tested and persuaded the EPA to attend a meeting where Victor presented their results. There he met Eric Stork, the man who seemed intent on keeping him from developing the car.

Eric Stork was head of EPA's Mobile Source Air Pollution Control Program, but he didn't seem to value this project at all. As regulator for the car industry, he spent a lot of time negotiating with motor manufacturers. Stork made it clear that he didn't want to rate the hybrid. Under pressure at the meeting, however, he agreed to continue with the testing the EPA was under contract to do.

▲ When the EPA rejected his plans for developing and testing a hybrid car, Victor Wouk calmly but persistently pursued his case through the National Science Foundation. Even with the support of the NSF, however, the EPA did not accept the idea that the hybrid's time had come.

◄ Victor Wouk with the Skylark at the EPA test site.

In 1974 the car was taken out to the EPA testing center at Ann Arbor, Michigan, and Wouk spent the time between tests chatting with the EPA's engineers. That's when he was told that his car would never pass the program, however well it did in the tests. "When we were near the end of the tests at the EPA, we had become very friendly with the engineers who were supervising," he said. "There was one who was particularly upset that we were sunk from the very beginning. Eric Stork had come in and said, 'Under no circumstances is the hybrid to be accepted.'" It seemed that the key official at the EPA was dead set against approving the hybrid car.

So Near and Yet So Far

Victor Wouk and Charles Rosen figured the Skylark hybrid had performed well in the tests, meeting the requirement to run with very low emissions. Victor measured them at about nine percent of those of a

The "Bad Guy"
Victor Wouk called Eric Stork "the bad guy" because he was unwilling to take the hybrid seriously. Stork was quoted saying about the work to test and purchase low-polluting vehicles: "It wasn't worth my time. It was just a nuisance. I was busy regulating the auto industry. I didn't have time for that Christmas tree ornament." He seems to have shared the view of the automobile industry that it would not be possible to produce a viable hybrid car. He also appears to have thought the government should have no role in developing such a vehicle for others to profit from.

> *"The project showed that a pair of determined individuals could use readily available and proved technologies to build quickly an HEV (Hybrid Electric Vehicle) that met the requirements of the Clean Air Act of 1970."*

- Victor Wouk, on pointing out that conventional automobiles did not start meeting EPA clean-air standards until 1986

gas-powered car—an incredible reduction. It was so close to the required performance, and he had also doubled the fuel economy of the Skylark compared to its standard performance.

Wouk was disgusted but not surprised when the EPA rejected his prototype in a report listing 75 faults. That sounds like a lot, but Victor responded to each fault, showing how it was irrelevant, exaggerated, or wrong. Part of the problem seems to have been that the tests were not geared to working on a hybrid. An electric car, almost by definition, produces no emissions, so how much pollution the hybrid produces when it switches between electricity and gas varies according to how it is driven and in what conditions.

But Eric Stork and the EPA would not change their minds about supporting the hybrid, and no one else would back it.

In 1976, after two years of letter writing and petitioning, Victor ran out of money to support the

► Two gas station attendants react to the sight of the array of batteries used to power this electric car. A conversion of a standard General Motors automobile, this car, called the Silver Volt, was produced by one of nearly two dozen electric car makers doing experimental work during the '70s.

project and gave up. He couldn't get the EPA to change its mind or get anyone else in the automobile business to fund the idea, and he had a family to feed. He was bitter about it, but he had to accept defeat. "By 1976 I was so disgusted, I lost so much energy, that I gave up," said Victor. It was the end of his hybrid.

The Electric Charge

One of the reasons the industry did not take up Victor's idea was that there was greater interest in electric cars. Between 1977 and 1979, General Motors spent more than $20 million trying to develop electric vehicles. One of the drawbacks, as Victor had said many years before, was battery performance. As a result, huge amounts of research went into developing a "super battery" that replaced lead acid with nickel hydride. The U.S. Advanced Battery Consortium spent more than $90 million on developing the "NiMH" battery in the 1990s.

These developments led to the hope that there may be a future for a viable electric car. It also contributed to further work on the hybrid, but that success story would be some years in the making.

▼ Victor always said that the greatest barrier to electric vehicles was the battery. This is the solution—the NiMH battery, which is far more powerful than its forerunners and has been used in the Toyota Prius and later hybrids.

Victor gave up on making a hybrid car himself, but he never gave up on the idea. He wrote letters and articles for newspapers and magazines, presented papers, and sat on numerous committees dealing with electrical technology, including how to lower greenhouse gas emissions.

In 1979, for example, he wrote: "Tests on, and studies of, hybrids have shown that petroleum usage of 80 miles per gallon (21 km/L) will be possible for normal daily driving, and 50 miles per gallon (80 km/L) when averaged over a year… We should start a crash program to commercialize the hybrid. It would make sense because all aspects of the hybrid have been proved workable. No new technologies need be developed." It seemed, however, that no one was interested.

Going Electric with Mass Transit

Victor was very involved in moves to introduce electric and electric-hybrid buses into city transit systems. He was a consultant when an all-electric bus fleet was introduced on Roosevelt Island in New York City. He argued for electric buses to be introduced (as opposed to electric trolley buses fed by overhead wires). The problem of how to charge the batteries was solved by a process called interim charging, in which they are

▲ In the years following his work on the hybrid, Victor Wouk served as a consultant helping many companies manage electricity. He was also involved with charitable and academic activities.

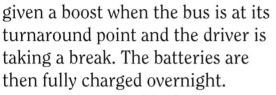

◀ Hybrid technology is perfect for buses, which do not usually travel at high speeds and can be recharged overnight or between runs. Hybrid electric buses now run on many city streets.

given a boost when the bus is at its turnaround point and the driver is taking a break. The batteries are then fully charged overnight.

In 1976, Dusseldorf, West Germany, decided to produce a line of 20 electric buses. Although the buses were more expensive, they were cheaper to run, required less maintenance, and lasted longer. As Victor pointed out in a letter about electric buses, "the social benefits of eliminating diesels with all the fume-belching, and airplane-jet-level sounds, is immeasurable. Ask residents of Roosevelt Island."

Victor continued to campaign for electric or electric-hybrid buses in New York. He got his point across. Today New York has North America's largest hybrid-electric bus fleet with nearly 700 vehicles.

See You in Court

Victor also acted as an expert witness in many court cases, particularly those involving the automobile industry. His main work, however, was as a consultant, advising companies on how they could use electricity effectively and, especially, on developing electric and hybrid vehicles.

▲ New York's famous yellow cabs spend a lot of time sitting in traffic, so the planned switch to an all-hybrid fleet makes a lot of sense. The 13,000-strong fleet of city taxis is being converted to hybrid (one of which is shown above). The target year for completion is 2012. It has been said that this change will have the same effect on improving air quality as removing 32,000 privately owned vehicles from busy streets.

A Man of Many Subjects

In addition to his business life, Victor gave talks and wrote letters non-stop on a huge range of subjects, reflecting his enormous enthusiasm for life and knowledge. In one such case, Victor addressed a conference on Lyme disease in the summer of 1987, despite having no medical qualifications at all.

Although they had an apartment in Manhattan, Victor and his wife Joy had a home in Millwood, a small village outside the city. They would go for walks in the woods and admire the local deer. Unfortunately these animals carried tiny creatures known as ticks that can give people a serious disease, and both he and his wife were bitten by them. He noticed a telltale rash early, and it was quickly treated. Joy suffered more and spent two weeks in a hospital being treated for Lyme disease caught from the bite.

Victor later spoke at a conference on the disease and wrote articles in an effort to inform doctors and the media about it. He also had a letter published in the *New York Times* advising people against wearing open sandals on lawns because the disease-carrying ticks can be carried from the deer by birds and rodents. Here was a prominent engineer advising the general public to wear sneakers and socks to avoid becoming sick!

▲ Beauty and the beast. Deer like these (above) can carry ticks (below). These tiny relatives of spiders, hugely magnified in the picture, can transfer disease as they feed on the blood of their host.

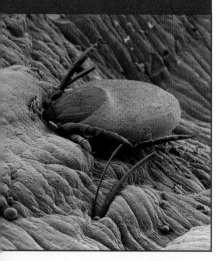

A Man in Demand

Victor was also closely involved with a charity, the Federation of Jewish Philanthropies, and continued his association with the academic community. In 2004 he gave Caltech all his papers. It is an amazingly large and varied selection of letters, patent applications, lectures, and talks.

Through all this, his interest in electric and hybrid cars was undiminished, and he saw politicians start to take a deeper interest in this technology. To his amazement, he also found that they did not think they could use his skills.

In 1993, President Bill Clinton set up the Partnership for a New Generation of Vehicles (PNGV), designed to get low-fuel-consumption, low-pollution cars and trucks onto U.S. roads. Victor heard about it in advance and knew he had information that would help. He wrote to one of the organizers, saying, "I would like to talk to you about this whole program. We've been through it in one form or another, and I can give you information that would save you years." He never got an answer to this or at least one other letter offering his help.

Three years later, the PNGV announced that it wanted to find the best type of hybrid. Victor went to a meeting about it at the Society of Automotive Engineers. "It was the only time I ever got up and asked an embarrassing question: 'Do any of you or your associates know about the Federal Clean Car Incentive Program?'" He was met with blank stares. He went on to ask if they had seen a recent article about how to make a better hybrid than his prototype. Again, no one had.

Talk to Me!

Victor Wouk summed up the PNGV: "I can point to six years of waste, doing studies, doing analyses

My Brother the Novelist
While Victor was building his reputation in the electronics industry, his brother Herman (shown above in 1962) was also making his mark. He had continued writing and had published several novels before the book that made his name was published in 1951. *The Caine Mutiny*, which drew on Herman's experiences in the navy during World War II, tells the story of how the crew of the USS *Caine* take over the ship from their captain because they think he has gone insane. Many of Herman Wouk's later books were bestsellers, and one even had a character based on his brother.

> *"He was immensely proud of it. He would take anyone for a drive at the drop of a hat, or sort of force you to ride with him regardless. The Taconic State Parkway was very near their country house and he would drive up and back for several miles including steep hills to demonstrate the car, bringing up and explaining the energy flow display."*
>
> - Victor Wouk's son Jordan, describing his father's enthusiasm for the Toyota Prius he had recently acquired

and tests and programs, and organizations trying to find out what the best vehicle would be." It seems remarkable that no one involved in the program thought to consult him. The PNGV folded in 2001, although some of its work was followed up by a government agency called Freedom Car and Vehicle Technologies (FCVT). In 2007, FCVT announced it was investing $20 million in plug-in hybrid vehicle research. Victor would have approved. He saw a great future for plug-in hybrids if they could be made to work.

One group of people did see the value in Victor's expertise—technicians in the Japanese car industry. Victor had contact with scientists from Honda and Toyota, who were very interested in his work and comments. In 1994, the president of Toyota told his staff it was time to develop a hybrid car. Three years later, they had one.

The Dream Becomes Reality

The Toyota Prius was the first mass-produced (and widely available) hybrid gas-electric car. Launched in Japan in 1997, it was available in the United States in 2001. One of the first customers was Victor Wouk. He was thrilled. His dream had finally come true.

▶ The Toyota Prius Hybrid attracted crowds at its unveiling in Japan in 1998.

The Prius uses an electric motor to start and move until it reaches about 25 miles per hour (40 km/h), at which point the gasoline engine starts up. If, however, the accelerator is pressed down hard when the vehicle has stopped, the gasoline engine kicks in right away, so the car is not sluggish. At other times, the electric motor and gas engine combine according to road conditions and type of driving.

Ever the scientist, Victor was interested in how Toyota had achieved this. "The major improvement that Toyota made was this continuously variable transmission," he said. "So you get absolutely smooth acceleration and this switching from one power to another—or to both—is almost 100 percent imperceptible to the driver." He felt this was due to an improvement in the way the car was put together, and not to any new technology in the concept of the hybrid. This is an important point, as it underlines his belief that had he gotten the go-ahead, he could have developed such a hybrid many years earlier.

Like all hybrid cars, the Toyota Prius uses regenerative braking, the system in which the energy used to slow the vehicle down is stored and fed back into the power system via the batteries. Victor Wouk played a major part in developing this idea, and today many major automobile manufacturers offer hybrid cars with regenerative braking.

▲ Workers at Japan's Toyota plant work to keep up with the demand for the Prius Hybrid in 2003. In one month alone, more than 17,000 orders were received for the new Hybrid.

The Wouk Lecture

In May 2005 the first Wouk Lecture, established by the family with the aim of showing the latest

▶ Central Park is an oasis of green and calm in New York. Victor Wouk lived nearby and understood the need for air to be clean enough for people to get out and enjoy it safely.

advances in science and technology, was given at Caltech. Victor was too ill to attend by then, but his son Jonathan rigged up a speaker by his bed so he could hear Erik Antonsson give a talk on advanced technology for space exploration. It seemed appropriate that the subject was about new frontiers. Furthermore, because of Victor's own passion for space travel, he must have felt very proud of this opening lecture. Three hours later, Victor died. Ironically, he was killed by lung cancer even though he never smoked and was active in the Citizens for Clean Air group that campaigned for air quality, including keeping smoking out of public places.

A Life Well Lived

A citation that Joy accepted on Victor's behalf for his work on hybrid systems only covers one part of Victor's extraordinary life and work, as we have seen.

It was a significant moment in 1974 when the EPA rejected Victor's highly rated Buick Skylark hybrid prototype. Nearly three decades later—when hybrid cars finally took their place on U.S. roads and highways—many facets were added to the life and work of Victor Wouk. And now this extraordinary man can at last be celebrated as the father of the hybrid car.

Chronology

1919	Victor Wouk is born on April 27 in New York City
1935–1939	Attends Columbia University in New York
1939–1941	Moves to Pasadena, California, and attends the California Institute of Technology as a graduate student. On June 15, marries Joy Lattman, whom he had met while going to college in New York
1941	Begins working for Westinghouse. He becomes part of a team of scientists working on the Manhattan Project, which leads to the development of the atomic bomb
1942	Awarded Ph.D. from Caltech
1944	Son Jonathan is born in May
1946	Forms the Beta Electric Corporation in suburban New York. Beta will become a leading provider of high-voltage electrical equipment.
1948	Son Jordan is born in October
1956	Sells Beta Electric Corporation and begins work for Sorensen
1959	Forms the Electronic Energy Conversion Corporation, which he later sells to Gulton Industries
1962	Tests the efficiency of the electric car for Russell Feldman, one of the founders of Motorola. He finds that the batteries are not powerful enough to run the car very fast or very long, but their potential as a supplemental source of power fuels Victor's own ideas about developing hybrid technology
1970	Clean Air Act is passed, setting emissions limits for motor vehicles. Victor sets up Petro-Electric Motors (PEM) for the purpose of developing a hybrid car
1972	With his business partner Charles Rosen, starts building the Buick Skylark hybrid
1974	Their hybrid car is tested and yet rejected by the Environmental Protection Agency
1976	Stops work on developing the hybrid car due to lack of funds and support and becomes an engineering consultant
1997	Toyota Prius is launched in Japan as the first widely available hybrid car
2004	Victor donates his papers to Caltech
2005	The Prius becomes widely available in the United States. Victor becomes an owner of one
2005	On May 19, Erik Antonsson delivers the first lecture in the Wouk Lecture series. Three hours later, Victor succumbs to cancer and dies

Glossary

aeronautics The science of flight, including how crafts are designed and made, and how to improve their performance

antenna A length of metal used for sending or receiving electronic signals

battery A device for storing electricity

carbon dioxide A greenhouse gas given off when fossil fuels are burned

continuously variable transmission A way of adjusting the gears in a car so that the engine runs efficiently, improving fuel economy and reducing exhaust emissions

electrical current The flow of electricity

electrical engineering The study of electricity, electronics, and electromagnetism

fossil fuels Fuels made from fossils—the remains of something that was once alive but has been dead a very long time. The three most important fossil fuels are coal, oil, and natural gas. All contain carbon, which is released when they are burned to form the gas carbon dioxide in the air

fuel consumption The amount of fuel, such as gasoline, that is used. Fuel consumption varies widely between different vehicles, but generally bigger engines require more fuel to run and therefore have a higher rate of fuel consumption

fuel efficient Using little fuel compared to other machines

global warming (or climate change) The gradual rise in temperature over the planet caused by the buildup of greenhouse gases in Earth's atmosphere. With this kind of climate change may come more extreme weather, such as storms and droughts, plus the raising of sea levels and melting of the polar ice caps and glaciers

greenhouse gas One of a group of gases that surround Earth and hold the heat in like a giant blanket. Without them, the planet would be too cold for life. Human activity is releasing more of these gases, which is raising the temperature on the planet

hybrid Something made up of two things or parts. For example, a hybrid car uses two sources of power, such as electricity and gasoline

interim charging Process in which batteries are given energy for a few minutes during a break in their use. Electric trolley buses use it to ensure that they have electricity available to power them back to their base, where the batteries are fully charged overnight

low emission Producing small amounts of pollutants. For example, a low-emission car will send out less harmful exhaust gases than one with a big and inefficient engine

mass production The manufacture of large quantities of goods on an assembly line in a factory. Carmaker Henry Ford was the first person to do this with his Model T Ford, the first car that was low enough in price that many people could afford to buy it

nickel-cadmium battery A type of rechargeable battery that provides more power than the lead-acid battery. Such batteries are now widely used for portable hand tools

NiMH battery A battery made using Nickel Metal-Hydride that can be recharged many times

patent The right given to an inventor to make, use, and sell his or her invention. A patent prevents other people from copying the idea

plug-in hybrid A hybrid car whose battery is recharged by being plugged into the electricity supply

pollution Harmful substances released into the environment. Pollution can happen naturally, as when a volcano erupts, or from human activity, such as a major oil spill or the excessive burning of fossil fuels

recharge To fill up a spent battery with electricity. Only certain batteries can be recharged

regenerative braking A process in which energy used to brake is stored for reuse. The energy generated by braking can be illustrated by stopping a free-spinning wheel with one's hand and feeling heat. This heat is energy created by movement. Regenerative braking captures this energy

solder To use a low-melting metal alloy, such as one made of lead or tin, to join together metals that require higher temperatures to melt and are less likely to fuse together

static electricity The electricity created when certain objects are rubbed together. Electric charges build up and can be released in the form of a spark or a small shock. Such a release can also have other results, such as making one's hair stand up

tenement An apartment building, usually fairly run down and rented to tenants cheaply

voltage The amount of "push" used to send electrons through a wire, forming an electric current

Further Information

Books

Coughlan, John. *Green Cars: Earth-Friendly Electric Vehicles* (Wheels). Capstone Press, 1994.

Juettner, Bonnie. *Hybrid Cars*. Norwood House Press, 2009.

Povey, Karen. *Hybrid Cars* (Our Environment), KidHaven Press, 2006.

Web sites

archives.caltech.edu
Use the search feature on this page from the Caltech archive for a number of photographs of Victor Wouk and his activities.

4wheeldrive.about.com/cs/buyacaronline/a/hybridcarstruck_5.htm
This site describes how hybrid cars work.

electricauto.org
The web site of the Electric Auto Association has information on the history and current developments of electric cars.

howstuffworks.com/hybrid-car.htm
This is another site that explains how hybrid cars work.

hybridcars.com/history/the-great-hybrid-car-cover-up-of-74.html
This article describes how Eric Stork of the EPA rejected Victor Wouk's plan to develop the hybrid car in the 1970s.

pluginamerica.org/links-and-resources/links.html
This site contains loads of information about plug-in technology.

Film

Who Killed the Electric Car?
Documentary about the battery-powered electric vehicle, written and directed by Chris Paine and featuring Tom Hanks and Mel Gibson. 2006.

Index

47

About the Author
Sean Callery is a writer and teacher specializing in children's books. He covers historical, science, and environmental topics.

Printed in the U.S.A. — CG